The Baby Analogy of Marriage

Howai K Thomas

The Baby Analogy of Marriage
Copyright © 2025 by Howai K Thomas

ISBN: 979-8992725407 (sc)
ISBN: 979-8992725414 (e)

Mission Wholelife Publications
941-467-0946
missionwholelifepublications.com
info@missionwholelifepublications.com

Table of Contents

Acknowledgment

The inspiration to write this book came about after preparing presentations for zoom meetings on self-worth, marriage and family life seminars, and the Spirit of God.

I'm far from being an expert on these subject matters and I don't have the perfect marriage either, but I am thankful for the materials of those who have impacted me tremendously and encouraged me to be a better person, husband and father.

However, I first want to give thanks to God for giving me the strength to endure the process and providing the needed resources.

Next, I want to especially thank my wife Kedine, and my son Timothy. They have been with me every step of the way and have sacrificed much family time so I can work on this project to its completion.

I also want to recognize a dear friend , Roland Mendonca, author of Living the Intentional Life, for not only encouraging and providing moral support but also reviewing my material and providing guidance where needed.

Another friend I would like to acknowledge is Petagay Williams. She invited me as a presenter on several zoom conferences. After which I realized that the materials I prepared had to be for a bigger audience. Thus I was given an opportunity to have a one-day seminar at my church. Thus was sparked a fire within me to continue speaking and writing on the subject of marriage and family life.

While none of this would have been a reality without God, none of it would have also been possible without my mother, Rosemarie Frith, whom I am also thankful to for growing me up with certain values and morally supporting me through my adult life.

To all my friends and family, thank you for all your support!

Introduction

According to the *New York Times*, 2022 was expected to be a "boom year for marriages," about 2.5 million weddings were anticipated to be held, which would be "the most since 1984—yet it's never been more difficult to plan one,"[1] the article went on to say.

While these individuals have their reasons for getting married, a 2019 Pew Research finding reported that "Among married and cohabiting adults, love is cited more than any other reason for why they decided to get married or to move in with their partner: 90% of those who are married and 73% of those living with a partner say love was a major factor in their decision."[2]

"At the deepest level, each of us desires someone to love and someone to love us in return—someone with whom we can share laughter, friendship, work, caring, and support through the good times as well as the hard times in life. People deeply desire this kind of relationship, but we also know that a great many couples don't achieve it."[3]

Among the reasons why many couples don't achieve this kind of relationship is not so much their personality differences; it's more so their confrontation or conflict management styles. In her book, *Confronting Without Offending*, Deborah Smith Pagues mentions four confrontation/conflict management personalities:

> While understanding how to resolve conflicts dramatically helps improve the togetherness in relationships, it takes time to develop a genuine friendship and a lasting relationship.

1. The Dictator: "Do it my way"

2. The Accommodator: "Have it your way"

3. The Abdicator: "I'll run away"

4. The Collaborator: "Let's find away"

Upon reading these, you might think that the Collaborator is the only one of the four that is the best conflict management style. While this is true, there *are* appropriate times to dictate, accommodate, or abdicate. Understanding when the time is right to do any of these is essential to harmony and unity in your relationships.[4]

While understanding how to resolve conflicts dramatically helps improve the togetherness in relationships, it takes time to develop a genuine friendship and a lasting relationship.

This especially applies to marriages because, in general, marriages go through different "seasons" and stages.

Of the five stages I've learned, the fourth and fifth are friendship and mature love. Though not every marriage progresses through the five stages identically or with the same intensity, it takes time, cooperation, patience, and persistence to endure the journey. See more on these stages in Chapter Five.

Besides the "birth" of marriages are the birth of babies, and within the last year (2022), approximately fifty percent more babies were born than weddings held. Many of them will grow up in a particular family structure, and the family is a basic unit of society.

> "The well-being of society, the success of the church, the prosperity of the nation, depend upon home influences.

This understanding is echoed in an article on Fox.com: "When architects design a building," it states, "they take special care to create a strong foundation onto which they can build a strong structure.

Family is the cornerstone of society — and if we want to build a strong society, we need to create strong families."[5]

In addition to this article, one writer brought this perspective into sharp focus when she wrote: "The well-being of society, the success of the church, the prosperity of the nation, depend upon home influences. The elevation or deterioration of the future of society will be determined by the manners and morals of the youth growing up around us."[6]

If you're an adult, you can attest that childhood upbringing shapes us for life. Through different interactions with parents or other caregivers, children learn the language of love and develop social skills such as affection, affirmation, compassion, gentleness, helpfulness, kindness, sensitivity, self-worth, and so on. On the other hand, children can also learn not-so-positive traits like apathy, indifference, insensitivity, selfishness, uncaring, unkindness, deceitfulness, dishonesty, and so on.

> "Yet, playing is not just for children but also for adults..."

While children are molded by their home life, a big part of their development is playing. Through playtimes, relevant social, emotional, and cognitive abilities are developed. Yet, playing is not just for children but also adults:

"Fun and play allow a release of oneself from all the pressures and hassles of being an adult. The relaxed togetherness of playful times is important in the initial development of the bond between two people. That's because when we are engaged in fun through play, we're often relaxed and more ourselves. It's under these conditions that people fall in love—when one sees in the other the relaxed self in the context of fun times together."[7]

This type of comparison is one of many that we'll look at, which can help us to see that the conception and birth of a child to adulthood illustrates the beginnings of marriage and the living out of married life to mature years. Thus, in this book, I will be using these comparisons as analogies for different aspects of relationships, marriage, and family life.

Furthermore, though this book contains and elaborates on certain vital relational concepts and principles, it serves as an introduction to the greater wealth of material available to help us grow and develop in our relationships, marriage, and family life.

Chapter One

Prenatal Care/Pre-Courtship

If you were to answer the question "When does prenatal care begin?" what would your answer be? Well, many years ago, I learned that prenatal care begins in the childhood days of a woman. As she goes through various stages of psychological, social, and physiological development, she is being prepared for the woman and mother she would become. So, prenatal care is more than multivitamins and medical checkups; it started with the health and wellness of mom in her childhood (even infancy), and continues into here adult years.

In fact, she, like all of us, becomes a depository of the culture and nurture she received, and all she has is what she has to give to her child or children.

Hence, the early years of our upbringing are crucial because they tend to influence our future lives and relationships including marriage.

Therefore, before a man or woman gets to a time of marriageability, they need a time of "self-preparation"— time enough to mature mentally, emotionally, physiologically, and socially, and the "early years" are a significant part of this process.

Who we are to become, we are now becoming, and once again, who we are is who we share with others.

In an upcoming chapter, we will talk about social circles and "sins of the fathers"[8] (generational curses, strongholds, or inherited tendencies), in which we will look at some of the impacts of childhood life on adult relationships.

Now, going back to the pre-preparation stage: As it is with a mother-to-be — that what she has is what she's got to give — so it is with individuals in any relationship: who they are is who they have to offer each other. Sure, we can learn and grow as the years go by, and we should; however, who we are to become, we are now becoming, and once again, who we are is who we share with others.

Self-Evaluation

So, who are you? Do you know yourself? Biblically, we are encouraged to "examine ourselves."[9] So, when was the last time you took an introspection of who you are — of the qualities and abilities you possess? For such self-evaluation, here are some questions to consider: Do

I have a good sense of self-worth, value, and self-esteem? In other words, how do you feel and think about yourself? Do you hate yourself? Do you see yourself as ugly, pretty, beautiful, or just a "plain old regular" person? In addition, are you concrete on your gender and sexual orientation? Do you constantly seek to be the center of attention? Are you always talking about yourself, comparing yourself to others, or name-dropping? These are just some of the questions to ask and answer of your self and your sincere answers to these vitally important questions reflect how you view yourself, and your self-perception will dictate to one degree or another your health and happiness, as well as the health and happiness of relationships you form, *especially* marriage.

Additionally, one sure way to disrupt harmony and bring instability into your life and marriage relationship is to not be resolute on the above questions prior to and during marriage. For such irresolution is double-mindedness, and a "double-minded person is unstable in all their ways."[10] Let's explore this thought some more.

Impact of Low-Self Esteem or Low Self-Image

Here are some more reasons to consider why understanding yourself matters significantly, personally and relationally. For example, if you don't think much of yourself— if you have low self-worth or self-esteem—then you'll lack confidence and proper motivation to strive for more or be more for your husband, wife, or other meaningful relationships. Besides this, you can even become very insecure or find yourself competing for or feeling unnecessarily threatened by others your spouse relates to.

Though a person who struggles with this kind of self-image is often abused, mistreated, and manipulated, ironically, they can become emotionally destructive to relationships.

Be careful, however, not to use such resources as a tool to control or manipulate your spouse to change.

If this describes you, it's wise to recognize and resolve it before you get emotionally tied to someone and marry them. If you are already married, you may be experiencing certain marital conflicts directly linked to your low self-image and may need to seek out some resources to help. You might even need to talk with a marriage counselor. If you're married to a spouse who struggles with low self-image or other emotional issues, you also might need some resources or counseling to help navigate your way in that relationship. Be careful, however, not to use such resources as a tool to control or manipulate your spouse to change.

Another aspect of the self-evaluation questionnaire that I want to elaborate on is the spirit of comparison—constantly comparing yourself to others to feel emotionally secure, or associating with certain people of notoriety to have value, self-worth or belonging. This is very superficial and emotionally unhealthy.[11]

While you may feel good "rolling with the big boys," and while it is perfectly ok to have positive role models, you will not have a strong sense of self-worth, value, and emotional security if you think you have to fit their mold—have what they have, live the lifestyle they live, or look how they look to be someone.

Instead of striving to fit the mold of those you admire or emulate to feel like you're someone of worth and value, focus more on moral, spiritual, intellectual, and recreational things to build up your personhood. Join a church outreach or community outreach program, learn a new skill, try some out-of-door recreation like gardening, biking, hiking or similar activities.

Once again, know and understand that your worth and value are not to be determined by the material, superficial things of this life.

Furthermore, a person's value and self-worth are not defined by their material possessions, contrary to conventional thinking.[12] Neither is your worth and value defined by how many vacations you can take, places you have been, the brand of clothes or shoes you wear, the type of vehicle you drive, where you live, or the kind of house you live in. However, this is not to say we shouldn't seek to raise our standard of life; on the contrary, because God endowed us all with intrinsic worth, we want to properly manage our resources to live the best, happiest, and healthiest quality life possible.

Once again, know and understand that your worth and value are not to be determined by the material, superficial things of this life. Who you are as a person matters more. Also, God has placed an infinite value on you.

Key Role of Parents or Primary Care Givers and Self-image

One final aspect I want to elaborate on is the key role of parents or primary caregivers in helping children develop a healthy self-image.

While both parents play a significant role in helping children develop a healthy self-image, research has found that the care and nurture a mother gives to her children, or a lack thereof, affect their overall well-being: "A mother's physical and emotional presence provides babies with two things: protection from stress and emotional regulation, both of which are important to healthy brain development and the child's future well-being."[13]

"Numerous studies also have found that children raised in a nurturing environment typically do better in school, and are more emotionally developed than their non-nurtured peers. Brain images have now revealed that a mother's love physically affects the volume of her child's hippocampus. In the study, children of nurturing mothers had hippocampal volumes 10 percent larger than children whose mothers were not as nurturing."[14]

In addition to the mother's care and nurture, father's profoundly impact their child's development, also. In short, various authorities on the subject of child development say that children with dads that are involved in their upbringing tend to be more emotionally-regulated, socially-adapted and do better academically than children with uninvolved or absentee dads. What's also incredible is that this positive impact is "felt" even throughout teen and adolescence.

"Moreover, studies have demonstrated that fathers contribute uniquely to their children's language and cognitive development. For instance, when dads engage positively during play or read to their children, it fosters stronger cognitive and language skills, sometimes even surpassing the impact of similar maternal behaviors."[15]

Validating your child is a positive way to boost their self-worth.

"Fathers also play a crucial role in pushing their children to take calculated risks, which can bolster problem-solving abilities and independence."[16]

As part of the nurturing process, validation plays a crucial role, also. Validating your child is a positive way to boost their self-worth. However, some parents tend to focus on their children's faults and seldom acknowledge their best efforts or things they do right. Rather than constantly correcting their children's mistakes only, parents should take the time to recognize and commend their children for their good behaviors. They should encourage them with words of approval and looks of love. "These will be as sunshine to the heart of a child and will lead to the cultivation of self-respect and pride of character." [17]

In addition to validating your child, parents also need to carefully consider how they administer discipline, as it can positively or negatively impact a child's emotional development. One writer on the subject puts it this way:

"Children are sensitive to the least injustice, and some become discouraged under it and will neither heed the loud, angry voice of command nor care for threatenings of punishment. Rebellion is too frequently established in the hearts of children through the wrong discipline of the parents, when if a proper course had been taken, the children would have formed good and harmonious characters."[18]

Understand, also, that rebellion in children can stem from various reasons, including excessive discipline or a lack of discipline and other underlying factors. It's possible that external factors, *"When I was a child, I spoke as a child, I understood as a child, I thought as a child: but when I became a man, I put away childish things."[19]* such as school, social media, church, or neighborhood, may be contributing to the situation and, you not aware of this.

So, as a parent, it's essential to consider your parenting methods but also investigate what external factors may be contributing to your child's rebellious behavior.

Common Courtesies to Be Developed Preparatory to Adulthood and Marriage

Another area in which parents play a crucial role in child development is in helping their children to adopt social etiquette. As a person grows from childhood through teenage years and into adulthood, they should have adopted certain social etiquette or common courtesies. To emphasize, one Bible writer said, *"When I was a child, I spoke as a child, I understood as a child, I thought as a child: but when I became a man, I put away childish things."*[19] This statement expresses the natural path to maturity, yet some adults have difficulty letting go of childish things. Regardless, here is a list of some common courtesies that should be adapted as we grow through childhood into mature adults. Some, if not the entire list, should be familiar to you.

1. If you drop it, pick it up.
2. If you made a mess, clean it up.
3. If you did wrong, say, "I'm sorry:" apologize.
4. If you are given something, say, "Thanks."
5. If you ask for something, say, "Please."
6. When you wake up, make your bed.
7. Wash your face and brush your teeth before facing the public.
8. Take showers daily.
9. Cover your coughs, burps and sneezes.
10. If you borrow it, bring it back.
11. If you move it, put it back.
12. If you broke it, get it fixed; if it isn't broken, don't fix it.

To be lacking in these and other social graces aren't minor matters. These find their expression in other areas of life, such as marriage, for example. Imagine having to clean up after a roommate, coworker, husband or wife, putting back everything they move or use, and dealing with smelly clothes and body odors daily. Also, imagine a spouse who has no consideration for how they hurt you. Think what it would be like if they don't care to have the car or household appliances repaired until they feel up to it. Not only does this sound like chaos, but gross immaturity and irresponsibility. Don't you think? Remember, as it is with a mother-to-be—that who she is, is what she has to give—so it is also with an individual; who they are is what they have to offer others.

Therefore, before thinking about saying, "I do," a person should already be cultured in certain common courtesies, manners, and morals, be settled in their identity, know what they want out of life, or at least have some idea about what they want, have a sense of self-worth and value, have good hygiene, have a sound spiritual foundation, have good money management and know how to interact with other people appropriately, so on and so on.

To be lacking in these and other social graces aren't minor matters.

Chapter Two

Conception of a Child/Courtship

Have you ever fallen in love? Love is a powerful emotion, though many are challenged to fully define it, we've often known when we've experienced it.

A 2019 Pew Research article reported that "Among married and cohabitating adults, love is cited more than any other reason for why they decided to get married or to move in with their partner: 90% of those who are married and 73% of those living with a partner say love was a major factor in their decision." [20]

> "Among married and cohabitating adults, love is cited more than any other reason for why they decided to get married or to move in with their partner..."

Still, many people can hardly wait to fall in love, get married, start a family, and live happily ever after.

However, many people have different conceptions, definitions and expressions of love. In fact, there are many types of love, including: Agape (selfless love), eros (romantic love), infatuation (love at first sight), ludus (childish or playful love), mania (obsessive love), philia/ phileo (friendship love), philautia (self-love), pragma (enduring love) storage (family love), and the list goes on.

But one way of defining the word "love" is: a choice to commit oneself emotionally, mentally, and physically to someone continually. In other words, it's "giving your all"—being fully-committed on every level necessary.

> Psychologists have concluded that the need to feel loved is a primary human emotional need.

Many relationships lack this type of love, yet if expressed and reciprocated, it would make the relationship more fulfilling. Now, how would you define the word "love?"

Our Lives are Riddled with This Four-Letter Word: Love.

However you would define it, love is essential to human relationships—our lives are riddled with this four-letter word. The following quotation elaborates on this idea:

"Love has a prominent, role in thousands of books, songs, magazines, and movies. Numerous philosophical and theological systems have made a prominent place for love. Psychologists have concluded that the need to feel loved is a primaryhuman emotional need. For love, we will climb mountains, cross seas, traverse desert sands, and endure untold hardships."[21]

Preparation is a Principle in Life

However, the idea of being in love and the hopes of marriage remind me of certain thoughts and emotions pregnant moms experience—like excitement, surprise, suspense, hopefulness, fear, curiosity, and concerns like, will it be a boy or girl? What type of personality will they have? Or, will this bond or break the household apart? And much more.

Regardless of the various emotions circulating through her being, both parents must prepare to properly care for that child when they are born. Such preparations may include baby-proofing your home; taking a childbirth/child care class; taking prenatal vitamins; packing a hospital bag; eating a healthy diet; researching your healthcare provider and childcare giver; getting baby essentials early; preparing the siblings for when the baby comes home; agreeing together on who is going to take turns day and night times to baby-care, and so on.

Preparation is a principle of life and is vital to successful parenting. Similarly, for marriage prospects: Getting married inadvisably, unwisely, or unpreparedly can bring you a tidal wave of misery. It can ruin your life, career, business, or reputation. Note the following sobering excerpt:

"No one can so effectually ruin a woman's happiness and usefulness, and make life a heart-sickening burden, as her own husband; and no one can do one hundredth part as much to chill the hopes and aspirations of a man, to paralyze his energies and ruin his influence and prospects, as his own wife."[22] Many men and women unfortunately have experienced this; some were fooled, some were naïve and others ill-prepared.

Things to Consider During Courtship—Before You Say, "I Do!"

In the previous chapter, we looked at pre-courtship—the before thinking about saying "I do" stage—a period of self-preparation. Again, it is vital to the success of marriage that individuals are in a "good place" psychologically, socially, and even spiritually before pursuing or considering a marriage prospect.

Here, I will present a category of things to consider in courtship—the before you say "I do" stage. Besides biblical principles, we will look at the importance of social circle, spirituality, and economics, mixed in with some practical points of view.

Don't Let Your Emotions Be Your Guide

When seeking a prospect for marriage, consult God first— pray about those whom you have an interest in. "Trust in the Lord with all your heart, and lean not to your own understanding, in all your ways acknowledge him and he shall direct your paths" is the divine counsel.[23]

Once, I contemplated "flipping cars," in the learning process, I was told not to get emotionally tied to any vehicle and that good deals always come along. If you are searching for or waiting on "Mr./Mrs. Right," do not allow your feelings to lead you on.

Additionally, regardless of how strong your feelings are for someone of interest, please do not follow your heart and dismiss the "red flags." Once again, emotions cannot be our only guide. Now, we can often spot "red flags" when we are unclear or uncomfortable with that person's behavior. Some examples of "red flags" are:

- Controlling behavior
- Discontented or depressive mindset
- Disregard for your personal or relational boundaries
- Inconsistent behaviors
- Jealousy issues
- Manipulation
- "Meltdowns" or angry outbursts
- Neediness
- Put-downs
- Self-centeredness
- And much more

A little side note: coming up in this chapter, you'll find some evaluation questions to help with the courtship process.

Regardless of how strong your feelings are for someone of interest, please do not follow your heart and dismiss the "red flags."

Please take note of them. If you are further along in your relationship, please get premarital counseling to help you figure things out (more on these as we go along).

Check Out Your Prospect's Social Circles

Besides consulting God and good reason, one checklist item to consider before you say "I do" is your prospect's social circle, even your own. One's social circle includes people they relate with often. Besides family members, this includes neighbors, co-workers, people at our schools, and even our place of worship.

One speaker on this topic, who I don't remember, said that how a person treats close family members, friends, neighbors, and coworkers are good indicator of who they are and how they would treat you. I know some circumstances may differ, and some people are pretentious (you always have those), but please take the time to evaluate them anyway. Look at whether they are respectful or not to their parents, neighbors, friends, and others in authority; also, consider how other people relate to them and use these as a barometer to gauge who you are getting involved with.

Coworkers: Another one to consider is whether they like their coworkers to do all the work while they "chill?" In other words, do they want to get all the benefits or the credits of other people's hard work rather than "pulling their weight" or doing their part?

Additionally, consider whether or not your prospect is a "taker" and not a "giver." Several biblical stories come to mind on this one: the woman at the well,[24,] the woman with the alabaster box,[25] and the wedding reception at Cana.[26]

For instance, the woman with the alabaster box of expensive perfume used it to anoint Jesus' feet to express her gratefulness for what He did for her. Ironically, she did this at a feast (party) that was in Jesus's honor, by Simon whom he cured of leprosy. In a similar manner, the woman at the well was one with low self-worth and lived an immoral life, but Jesus gave her hope and restored her worth. She, in turn, published Him abroad, which helped him in the fulfillment of His mission of seeking and saving broken, hurting people. Added to these, is the wedding reception at Cana. When they ran out of wine, Jesus worked a miracle to give them fresh wine, which saved the host from embarrassment.

Does your prospect add value to others, or do they only relate to others to get what they can from them?

In all of these scenarios, we find Jesus pouring into other people's lives, and they, likewise, into His.

So, again, I ask, does your prospect add value to others, or do they only relate to others to get what they can from them? Are they a "taker" and not a "giver?" Then, after answering, ask yourself, "Would this person add value to or take value away from my life?"

Friends: It's readily understood that friends are a major part of one's social circle. It is said that opposites attract; however, when it comes to friends, similarities are what attract. Hence, the saying: "Show me your friends, and I'll tell you who you are." In general, this is true. As much as the saying: "birds of a feather flock together" is also true. Now, this is not about judging a person but evaluating behaviors and relational connections to understand them better. So, if you get to know the friends, you can get a perspective of that person that you might not get otherwise.

For example, suppose a prospect (boyfriend or girlfriend) falls in line with their friend's activities, whether they are unwholesome, immoral, or illegal, rather than saying no or staying away. In this case, others easily influence them; they bend easily under peer pressure and are more of a follower and not a leader.

This may also help you see emotional insecurities that can potentially be emotionally destructive to a relationship together.

It might even be that you're the person to help them get help with identity, belonging, and perhaps other emotional issues they are struggling with. If this is the case, then help, but don't get emotionally entangled with such a person while helping; be clear on what your intentions are. Also, include at least one more trusted person to assist you, and allow healing and restoration to occur in that person's life;

then, they can better see where they want to go with life and intimate relationships.

Parent-child relationship: Earlier, I mentioned that how a person treats their parents reveals who they are and how they would behave toward you, generally speaking. However, the way a person is treated by their parents, and other family members also impresses upon them a particular social culture, which, in turn, influences how they relate to their parents, their own family, and others.

While many of them grow up to become outstanding citizens, husbands, wives, fathers, or mothers and lead fulfilling careers, some carry emotional scars and baggage from their childhood. As a result, they have a hard time forming emotionally healthy relationships. Thus, knowing about your prospect's family relations and childhood is very important. This is not to say their parents, other family members, or caregivers are responsible for their actions or choices. Our actions and choices are *our* actions and choices, no one else's. So are the results that come from them. However, the reality is that these social dynamics do influence a person's behavior to one degree or another.

Generational Curses, Strongholds, or Inherited Tendencies

To reiterate: Our childhood upbringing impacts our future life and relationships because "by beholding (things which we are exposed to or experience) we become changed,"[27] even by the same spirit operating in those who deeply mold our lives.

For example, A man gets married and starts a family with the desire not to be angry and abusive like his parents were to him. Yet, to his dismay, he "blows up" at his wife or his children. He might even become withdrawn from them when they continually misbehave. Now, he may say to himself, "I am just like my parents," even though his parents might have been worse than he.

What this man is experiencing is what I call the "sins of the fathers" syndrome (generational curse, stronghold, or inherited tendency). These are the traits we've inherited and cultivated (or nurtured), which we carry with us into our family relations and others; like bad genes, when triggered, we express them in our attitudes and behaviors. They are so deeply rooted in us that, as much as we desire not to express them, at times we do; this is not to say that we can't stop or change; we can. We also may desire not to make the same mistakes our parents and their generation have made, but we find ourselves making them anyway or going to the other extreme. Hence, a knowledge of wrong and a desire to change is a great start, but it's not good enough equipment to be a better person, husband, father, wife, or mother; it's not enough to break the cycle of bad habits or strongholds.

Even though we can identify relationship problems, we can still fall prey to them, and again, at times, we do. Unless we have some re-education or transformative experience, we are likely to make the same mistakes and live life in the same manner as how we were brought up, or we might, once again, swing the pendulum to the other extreme and do worse in a different way. Even I can identify this in my generation and succeeding generation's marriages and family lives.

Also, take a look at the kings in the Bible and how the poor choices of one father-king deathly affected many generations. For example, King Jeroboam's son, grandson, great-grandson and great great-grandson, and others, followed in King Jeroboams footsteps, leading a nation into decades of immorality. This demonstrates to us that, like the one bad apple which spoiled the whole bunch; so one cherished, inherited or cultivated family trait can wreck havoc in a family or a nation for many generations. (see 1Kings chapters 15 &16; 2 Kings chapter 15).

The "sins of our fathers" also remind me of bad habits. Which is also something to observe in your prospect and not to be overlooked. Habits are formed throughout our growing-up years and are hard to break, especially the bad ones—though they *can* be broken.

Typically, a person's habits tend to strengthen with age; hence, those habits grow stronger throughout marriage, people don't just grow out of it. I'm a witness to this one. I've been married for fifteen years and have experienced how easy it

It requires a willingness to change, prayer and fasting, the grace of God, and dedication to practicing good habits to break the cycle of the "sins of the fathers" is to default to certain habits and behaviors rather than consistently maintaining certain good ones. While bad habits can be broken, know that they can cause unnecessary hurts and growing pains in relationships, but more so in a lifelong commitment, such as marriage.

Among other things, it requires a willingness to change, prayer and fasting, the grace of God, and dedication to practicing good habits to break the cycle of the "sins of the fathers" (the cycle of hurtful habits, inherited tendencies, generational curses, or strongholds.)

Seek Premarital Counsel

Another thing you need to do to help you navigate the contours of courtship is to seek counsel. For without good counsel, any endeavor, including marriage, will fail, but in the multitude of good counsel, there is wisdom, safety, and plans that can be better established.[28] If you're planning on getting married, don't do so without taking premarital counseling. If you got married without getting premarital counseling, you might require some. For those who plan to get married, before you go to formal counseling, talk to those who know and often relate to the person you're interested in or you're already courting. It is often said that we are blinded by our own emotions when we have a deep interest in someone. Usually, others are better able to help us get a proper perspective of that person, just as others are also better able to help us see ourselves because, indeed, we have self-perception biases.

> For without good counsel, any endeavor, including marriage, will fail,

Your Prospect's Religious Beliefs

Besides considering your prospect's social circle, you want to understand their spiritual perspectives. For, how "can two walk together unless they are agreed?"[29] one bible writer asks. In other words, how can two people maintain a committed, harmonious relationship if they live two different, conflicting lifestyles or live by two different religious bases?

Many people govern their way of life by their religious beliefs. For example, the things they do or don't do, the type of entertainment they prefer, places they go or don't go to, the music they listen or don't listen to, and movies they watch or don't watch; these and other lifestyle choices are usually based on some religious philosophy (even for those who don't profess religion). Understanding this helps to avoid unnecessary conflicts and misunderstandings about certain preferences they have or choices they make.

As you find out what their religious beliefs are, ask how similar or different their beliefs are to yours. Also, if you both were to commit to a lifelong relationship together, would the different beliefs jeopardize your union?

> Besides considering your prospect's social circle, you want to understand their spiritual perspectives.

Furthermore, If husbands and wives have very different beliefs, they will inevitably experience division and disruption of spiritual harmony in the home directly related to those different religious beliefs. Often, children raised in this type of home grow up with conflicting religious standards, and many rebel against or abandon Bible standards. Often, those who remain in the faith perpetuate the same spiritual dysfunctionality they experienced in their parents' home. This is one of the injuries of "unequally-yoked" marriages, which, by the way, can also occur among members of the same faith and not just with those who marry and have children with someone of a different religion. This is even the more proof that you must be diligent about choosing someone to marry.

Additionally, you want to get an idea of your potential spouse's spiritual maturity so you can know how to better relate to them.

Another thing to consider about your person of interest is how they live outside of church. Regular church attendance is good; however, Christian-living outside the four walls of the church is a better reflection of a person's religious convictions (See James 1:27; 3:12-14).

For instance, if they have regular daily devotions, Bible studies, and outreach, this indicates that they take personal interest and responsibility for their own spiritual growth, which is also good preparation for the spiritual leadership of Christian fathers and husbands. Additionally, you want to get an idea of your potential spouse's spiritual maturity so you can know how to better relate to them.

So, if you are interested in or married to a new believer, for example, you will need to be more patient with them as they continue to learn and grow in their "walk" with Christ. Therefore, it is unrealistic to expect them to behave and speak in mature Christian terms and concepts as fluently as you or other mature Christians do.

On the flip side of the coin, a new believer will also have to learn to accommodate being married to a more mature believer. This may also mean working out how you want to proceed with family worship, personal study time, mission trips, or other spiritual endeavors, as you both will have a different spiritual capacity and temperament.

Much of what I just said also applies to couples who have a big age gap between them. Think of it as two siblings in a household; one of them in elementary and the other in high school. While there are some common subjects they will both study, the educational levels of the two are vastly different; likewise, their emotional and social development, and life experiences. So it is with age-gaped couples: Generally speaking, their maturity levels, the time period in which they grew up, and their life experiences differ widely and compound the typical relationship challenges couples encounter.

Finances/Money Management

Besides knowing the social circle and spiritual life of the one you are interested in courting, or, perhaps, you're *already* courting, you should also know about their economics (money management and financial goals). It is noted that bad financial management is one of the main things that destroys marriages. I've heard of spouses who gamble their savings or family property away. But besides this, it can lead to bad debt, bankruptcy, overreliance on credit, homelessness, domestic abuse, and other relationship ills. Ironically, a love affair with money is also harmful to relationships and not just the mishandling of it.

So, before you say "I do!" Here are some evaluation questions to consider regarding finances/money management:

1. Do they save, or do they spend every dollar they get?

2. Are they willing to work a job, even if it isn't what they've trained for until they get into their career field?

3. Do they still depend on their parents to finance them?

4. Do they budget according to their preferences or what they can afford?

5. Do they work and blow their wages on parties, "brand-name" items, and weekend vacations?

6. Do they do unscrupulous, unethical, or unlawful things to gain money?

7. Do they practice tithing?

8. Are they an honest worker?

9. Luke 16:10 says, "Faithfulness in the least is faithfulness in much." So, how do they treat entry-level jobs, small tasks, or small projects?

10. What do you observe about their attitude towards these duties?

11. Are they humble or prideful to perform these and other menial duties if required by their employer?

Here is something to remember: faithfulness is an essential quality to look for in a prospect to marry—faithfulness, even in menial duties.

Aside from the three above things to observe in your prospect for marriage, the following checklist items are also vital to consider and discuss: sleep habits, eating habits, goals and vision, who is expected to fulfill which roles and responsibilities, parenting, sexual experience and expectations, place of residence and worship, and so on. A few reasons why these and others are critical to talk about before marriage is that they help to avoid unrealistic expectations and unnecessary conflicts. This leads to peace and harmony in the marriage union.

Finally, "examine carefully to see if your married life would be happy or inharmonious and wretched. Let the questions be raised, Will this union help me heavenward? Will it increase my love for God? And will it enlarge my sphere of usefulness in this life? If these reflections present no drawback, then in the fear of God move forward."[30]

> Faithfulness is an essential quality to look for in a prospect to marry—faithfulness, even in menial duties.

Chapter Three

Childhood/ Married Life

It is generally understood that the first three years of any newly-found organization (business, academic, or social) are strong indicators of their future failure or success. So it is with childhood and marriage.

The birth of a child comes with waves of emotions and different kinds of interactions (excitement, attentiveness, nurture, tender moments, little affections, affirmation, helpfulness, curiosity, learning and bonding, compassion, funny times, fear, playfulness, sacrifice, meeting physical and emotional needs, etc.). Some of these baby interactions mirror the five love languages of relationships. Before getting into that, however, let us first look at the early years of a child and see how this illustrates some aspects of the early marriage years.

Early Years Are Foundational

Within the period of birth to seven years of age character is formed, and the first three years of a child's life are crucial to their continued growth and development. In these years, if there is malnutrition or lack of proper nurture, the child will experience developmental challenges. So it is with marriage: Much of the joys and struggles experienced therein result from the foundation upon which the marriage was laid in the early years.. "It is from the marriage hour that many men and women date their success or failure in this life, and their hopes of the future life."[31]

So, for example, a marriage that starts out and continues with good qualities such as honesty, open communication, trust, and transparency will have much fewer issues than one of controlling behavior, dishonesty, poor communication, and lack of transparency.

One thing that tests that foundation, though, is the addition of a child/children. It is typical for newlyweds to start having children in the first year of marriage, and many are encouraged to do so as soon as they get married. However, just as mothers bond with their

It is also essential that newlyweds spend the first-years bonding and building a firm foundation to withstand the vicissitudes of life children in the early years, so it is also essential that newlyweds spend the first-years bonding and building a firm foundation to withstand the vicissitudes of life (including parenting).

Interestingly, I read in the Bible that in ancient Jewish culture, newlyweds would get a one-year "marriage leave". It's kind of like a one-year-honeymoon experience in which time, both the husband and his wife would spend time learning and bonding with each other.

Adaptability and Flexibility: Two Vital Factors

While the addition of a child/children affects how roles, responsibilities, and schedules are fulfilled. Both childcare and marriage maintenance require adaptability and flexibility to make it through. Of course, this doesn't mean you'll have an issue-free parenting or marriage experience. Each of these types of relationships come with unique challenges, especially if you were always catered to, and you did not have to bear much responsibility in the caretaking of home-life or another person. However, moving with the ebb and flow of life, and not only parenting or marriage, makes life's journey more manageable and rewarding.

Moving with the ebb and flow of life, and not only parenting or marriage, makes life's journey more manageable and rewarding.

So then, adaptability and flexibility are two necessary factors in marriage maintenance: "those who are not willing to adapt themselves to each other's disposition, so as to avoid unpleasant differences and contentions;"[32] "who handle their differences and conflicts poorly with put-downs and hostility and harsh views of one another, are the most likely to develop serious problems."[33]

This doesn't mean that one should yield to every desire, request, or demand of the other person for there to be peace, unity, and harmony. That is narcissistic and emotionally destructive to marriages, to say the least. No one personality should dominate and control the mind of the other or the marriage. There is to be a sense of mutual honor, humility, respect, and mutual submission.

In a simple sense, what the above excerpt is saying is that for relationships to go forward and be mutually beneficial, there has to be adaptability and flexibility—a give and take—some kind of compromise has to be made. Be careful, though, not to compromise on certain values and principles so that you don't lose your self-worth and self-respect, nor diminish the self-worth and self-respect of the other person by such compromises. To do so would jeopardize the integrity of the marriage, and the health, happiness, and security of the husband and wife will be at stake.

Let's now look at some other vital aspects of marriage that relates to the early growing-up years.

Below is a relisting of the relational dynamics mentioned at the beginning of the chapter. Again, notice how they mirror the five love languages:

- Talking to and giving a child undivided attention = Quality Time

- Physical Affection like rubbing hands, faces, feet, or hugging and kissing = Physical Touch

- Providing toys, games, and other fun gifts = Giving Gifts

- Terms of endearment like "cutie pie," "munchkin," "sunshine," "my little champion," and others = Words of Affirmation

These are bonding and nurturing activities that unify hearts and minds.

For married couples, bonding and uniting can, at times, be daunting; yet, it's when husbands and wives are united in the "bonds of peace" that they feel more secure in each other's love and experience deeper intimacy, and a greater sense of marital satisfaction.

The Five Love Languages

Going back to the love languages interactions, Gary Chapman, the author of *The 5 Love Languages*, puts forth the concept that everyone has at least one primary love language.[34] When it is spoken, it speaks more deeply to their emotions and fills up that person's "love tank."

According to Mr. Chapman, the five love languages are:

It's when husbands and wives are united in the "bonds of peace" that they feel more secure in each other's love and experience deeper intimacy,

1. "Words of Affirmation"[35]
2. "Acts of Service"[36]
3. "Receiving Gifts"[37]
4. "Quality Time"[38]
5. "Physical Touch"[39]

Here is an introduction to these love languages from one of his books:

> ***Words of Affirmation***—Using words to provide affirmation to your spouse. "You look nice in that dress." "I really appreciate what you did for me." "Do you know one of the things I like about you? Your smile. When you smile at me, the whole world looks beautiful." "One of the things I like about you is your integrity. I know that you will always tell me the truth." The words may focus on how they look, something they have done for you, or some personality trait. You are simply using words to express your love. You can speak the words, write the words, or even sing the words. Remember the ancient Hebrew proverb we quoted in Chapter 1? "The tongue has the power of life and death."
>
> You are simply using words to express your love.
>
> For some people, Words of Affirmation is their primary love language. If you give them affirming words, they thrive. They feel deeply loved. If,

on the other hand, you give them harsh, critical words, it is like a dagger in their heart.

Acts of service—Doing something for your spouse that you know they would like for you to do. Cooking a meal is an act of service. Washing dishes, folding towels, watering the lawn, washing the car, or changing the baby's diaper are all acts of service. The husband whom I described earlier was speaking this love language. Many wives would feel deeply loved if their husbands did those acts of service. His problem was that he was not married to one of these women. Acts of Service was not his wife's love language. He was, in fact, expressing love, but it was missing the target.

Have you heard the old saying, "Actions speak louder than words?" That is true if Acts of Service is your love language. However, it is not true for everyone.

Receiving Gifts — It is universal to give gifts as an expression of love. My academic background before I studied counseling was cultural anthropology, the study of cultures. We have never discovered a culture where gift giving is not an expression of love.

The gift says to the recipient, "They were thinking about me. Look what they got for me."

The gift need not be expensive. I have sometimes suggested to husbands that they follow the example of their young children who pick dandelions in the yard and give them to their mothers. I'm not suggesting dandelions, but flowers from the yard. If you don't have flowers in your yard, look at your neighbor's yard. (Ask your neighbors, don't steal them.) One husband told me that he was taking a walk and saw a bird feather. He picked it up and took it home and gave it to his wife with these words: "Honey, I found this feather while I was walking, and I thought of you. You are the wind beneath my wings, girl, and I love you." He hit a home run because his wife's primary love language was Words of Affirmation, and her secondary language was Receiving Gifts.

If Receiving Gifts is your spouse's primary love language, I suggest you make a list of the kind of things in which they show interest.

Quality Time—Giving your spouse your undivided attention. I do not mean sitting on the couch watching television (something else has your attention.) Nor do I mean sitting in the same room while both of you are looking at your laptops. I'm talking about things like sitting on the couch or in your favorite chairs, with the television off, computers down, not answering your phones, but rather looking at each other and talking and listening. They have your undivided attention.

Or taking a walk and talking as you walk. Or, in your former life, it might have been going to your favorite restaurant, assuming that you were talking and listening to each other. (Maybe that day will return soon.) I have been amazed in the past several years to observe couples sitting in the restaurant with both of them on their smartphones. I hope neither of their love languages is Quality Time.

What you are doing is not as important as the fact you are doing it together.

Quality time also has other dialects, such as doing something together that at least one of you enjoys doing and the other chooses to participate. For the person whose love language is Quality Time, what you are doing is not as important as the fact you are doing it together. It may be planting a garden together. During this season, it may be cleaning out a closet or the garage together. The important thing is that you are choosing to give your full attention to being with your spouse.

It may be planting a garden together. During this season, it may be cleaning out a closet or the garage together. The important thing is that you are choosing to give your full attention to being with your spouse.

Physical Touch—Meaningful, affirming touches. In a marriage, this would be such things as holding hands, kissing, embracing, sexual intercourse, placing your hand on their shoulder as you pour their coffee, or putting your hand on their leg as you drive down the road. We have long known the power of physical touch. That is why we cuddle babies in our arms, and long before the baby understands the meaning of love, the baby feels loved by physical touch.

Out of the five love languages, each of us has a primary love language. One of them speaks more deeply to us emotionally than the other four. We can receive Now, don't assume that all men have Physical Touch as their primary love language. love in all five languages, but one is more meaningful. It is similar to spoken language. Each of us grew up speaking a language with a dialect. That is the one we understand best. We call it our "native tongue." The same is true with love. Some people have said to me, "I think I have two love languages." My response is, "Fine, we will call you bilingual." However, most people have one that is predominant.

Now, don't assume that all men have Physical Touch as their primary love language. I say this because so many men will automatically say, "I know my love language—Physical Touch." They are talking about sexual intercourse. My question to them is, "Do non-sexual touches make you feel loved?" At first, they look at me like a deer in the headlights as if to ask, "Are there non-sexual touches?" Then I ask, "Let's say the two of you are taking a walk, and your wife reaches out and holds your hand. Does that make you feel loved?" If they say, "No, that kind of irritates me when I'm walking." "So," I asked, "let's say she is pouring you a cup of coffee, and she puts her hand on your shoulder. Does that make you feel loved?" If he says, "Not really." "Well then, Physical Touch is not your love language. You like sex, but touch is not your love language."

The love languages are not gender specific. A man or a woman can have any one of the five as their primary love language. The important thing is to discover your spouse's primary love language and choose to speak it on a regular basis. This does not mean that you can ignore the other languages. No, you can sprinkle in the other four for "extra credit." However, if you don't speak your spouse's primary love language, they will not feel loved even though you are speaking some of the other languages.[40]

Conflicts & Differences

Inevitably, even while speaking our spouse's love language, We will experience conflicts in marriage as we do in any kind of human relationship. Just as it is with a growing child, misunderstandings and disagreements bring conflicts. Usually, the child is the one with the misunderstanding and their desires conflict

Ultimately, the parent has to hold the reigns.

with the rules and regulations of the parent. For instance, the child thinks he should always hear yes and not no when he asks for a cookie or some tasty snack. Sometimes, the misunderstanding comes because the parent says yes when they should say no or has been saying yes but now decides to say no, and the child doesn't understand why the sudden change of mind. Sometimes, the child throws a tantrum because he wants to have his own way, regardless of what mom or dad thinks or says. Ultimately, the parent has to hold the reigns.

Marriages also experience these disagreements and misunderstandings. "By contention over trivial matters a bitter spirit is cultivated. Open disagreements and bickering bring inexpressible misery into the home and drive asunder those who should be united in the bonds of love."[41]

At times, it's when trying to work out their differences to maintain harmony, peace, and oneness, couples end up arguing with one another, but some couples say they can't remember ever arguing.

Before I got married, I desired that this would be my marriage. It didn't take long after being married to find out that it won't be. In fact, my wife and I still have arguments, and I'm amazed at how easily they get started at times. Sometimes, it's over the most trivial things.

Is it wrong for married couples to argue, though? This is what an excerpt from *Psychology Today* has to say about arguments.

> Arguments aren't necessarily a bad sign. It means differences are surfacing, but in some relationships, differences aren't acknowledged. This
>
> Resolving disagreements in a healthy way creates understanding and brings couples closer together.
>
> may be because either one partner dominates, or because both individuals are merged and don't really know themselves. One or both partners may be sacrificing who they are to please the other. These solutions to differences usually backfire, because they build resentment and passive-aggressive behavior, and closeness and intimacy suffer.[42]

The same article goes on to talk about conflicts being normal in relationships, and resolving them positively should be the goal.

> "It's normal to have conflict in relationships." It says. "People are different, and their desires and needs will inevitably clash. Resolving disagreements in a healthy way creates understanding and brings couples closer together.

The objective should be the betterment of the relationship. This is positive conflict." [43]

When seeking to resolve conflicts, here is a couple of key things to keep in mind:

1. Choose to resolve, rather than dissolve, conflicts. While, at times, it's best to address a problem the same day, sometimes it is necessary to wait a couple of hours or days to address it, especially when emotions are high. Do not let issues go unresolved for too long, though. They can fester and become volcanoes. Depending on the impact of the issue on the relationship, however, would determine how soon it should be addressed. One of the things I have learned recently is that even if you cannot settle the conflict on the same day, you can still say, "I am sorry . . ." Then, the next day, seek to resolve the conflict.

2. To resolve conflicts and maintain unity, choose confrontation instead of retaliation. In her book, Debra Paget Smith talks about the concept of *Confronting Without Offending.* She makes it clear that we should confront people when there is an issue affecting the relationship and that the word *confront* "means to stand or meet face-to-face," [44] not antagonism. So, when we confront someone, the goal is to make wrongs right so that we can

    "Do it Prayerfully, Promptly, Personally, Privately, and Purposefully." [45]

be reconciled with that person (see Matt. 5:23-24; 18:15). There are five "P's" that Debra talks about when confronting without offending. She says, "Do it Prayerfully, Promptly, Personally, Privately, and Purposefully."[45] All of these are found in Jesus's teaching on confrontation and can be applied to different types of relationships.

3. When we take the above approaches to resolving conflicts, we are also learning how to have winsome arguments, which involves:

    1. Attacking the issues and the problems, not the person.

    2. Owning your wrongs.

    3. Speaking "verbal balms" instead of "verbal bombs,'" which are kind, loving, affirming words instead of harsh, cruel, and condemning words.[46]

4. Exercise forgiveness and reconciliation.

    a. Confess your faults one to another and pray for each other; it makes room for healing and reconciliation.

    Then make peace, for peace-making fosters right doing (see James 5:16; 3:18).

In addition, please see Appendix A, which has ten pointers for marriage maintenance.

Chapter Four

Youth and Teen/Individuality in Marriage

One vital key about the growing-up years is an awareness of developmental stages. Before we become adults, we go through different stages of development. In the middle and teen years, we go through various psychological and physiological changes. For example, though we develop ninety-five percent of our adult brain by age six and one hundred percent by age seven,[47] it goes through a process of "remodeling" during the teenage years. During this period, our amygdala is very active and often influences our behaviors, which, at times, can be impulsive and even irrational; so, we tend to make decisions more from feelings rather than proper reasoning.

Like teens, married couples can sometimes experience different waves of emotions. Sometimes, these emotions are from bad life experiences resulting from poor choices, remorse or regret for missed opportunities, the loss of employment, a friendship, a loved one, or just "life taking its course." Even couples sometimes have more conflicts because they act purely out of emotions, and their impulsive, irrational behaviors injure the marriage.

While contemplating that individuals and marriages go through different phases that affect our relationships, I came across another book by Gary Chapman titled *The 4 Seasons of Marriage*. I was surprised to find this book, and it expanded my mind on the idea that individuals and marriages go through different seasons. "Marriage relationships are constantly changing." He writes. "Attitudes shift, emotions fluctuate, and the way spouses treat each other ebbs and flows between loving and not loving."[48]

> Like teens, married couples can sometimes experience different waves of emotions.

The challenge Is to maintain composure regardless of our emotional wavelength.

It has become popular in Western culture over the past forty years to exalt emotions as the guiding light that determines our actions. After more than 30 years of counseling couples, I am convinced this is a misguided notion. Don't misunderstand me: I am not suggesting that emotions are not important. Emotions tell us that something is wrong or right in a relationship, but emotions must lead to reason, and reason must be guided by truth if we are to take constructive action. We must not short-circuit the process and jump straight from emotions to action without the benefit of reason. Many couples who have done this have found themselves in winter when they could have ended up in spring or summer.[49]

H.A.L.T.

Furthermore, it is understood by many that when emotions are high, intellect is low. Therefore, it is not good to make major decisions in this state of being. Instead, wait until your emotions calm down, then "tackle" the issues or make life-altering decisions.

To emphasize this further, many years ago, I learned an acronym called H.A.L.T. The idea is not to make major or life-changing decisions when you're hungry (H), angry (A), lonely (L), or tired (T). I have used this on many occasions, and it has helped me tremendously in maintaining marriage, ministry, and managing the vicissitudes of life. I hope you can benefit from it, too!

Another aspect of the teenage years that reflects on marital relationships is puberty. While enduring puberty, we seek to express our personalities more and desire to be more independent and autonomous from our parents. Although, we are not yet adults and aren't fully ready for adult-life responsibilities. However, let us be careful not to treat teens as little children, and that we make room for them to gain and express their independence responsibly, which is crucial to becoming and managing adult life well.

One hindrance to this process is that some parents believe in treating children equally, that everyone should be included in every activity, regardless of the age difference of the siblings. But, when you have children of different ages (like teens and toddlers), this isn't a good practice since they are of different emotional maturity and at varying levels of development.

Such an approach can also lead to ill feelings among siblings because teens need some personal space to do teens things and not be subjected to toddler world.

Likewise, toddlers and young children need space to be such. It's unrealistic and emotionally unhealthy for them to participate in everyone's activities. They may feel a little left out sometimes, but that's a part of the growing-up process and the path to maturity.

> Toddlers' needs differ from that of preteens and teenagers; treat them accordingly.

The child may misunderstand this as "unfair treatment," but you, the parent, must reinforce healthy boundaries.

So, as parents, we not only need to pay attention to the different personality traits in our children but also understand that as they grow and develop, their emotional and social needs change. Therefore, what's appropriate for one age group will not be appropriate for another.

Toddlers' needs differ from that of preteens and teenagers; treat them accordingly.

Not only do parents need to have this understanding, but also married couples as they relate to one another. It is a fact that the more time we spend together, the more we bond; however, while many spouses do many things together, they each need some personal, alone time for their own mental wellness—time for introspection, personal thought, personal devotion, personal care, or even hobbies. Also, while couples should be friends, they need friends besides each other, not just guys or girls to "hang out with," but friends who have their best interests at heart, who serve as accountability partners and a part of their support network.

Leading by Example

One additional thought regarding teenagers or children is that to help them meet your expectations, fulfill duties, and develop well; they need standards to live by. For example, if you want them to be neat and tidy, show them what neat and tidy looks like, and be neat and tidy yourself. If you want them to be dutiful, demonstrate what it means to be dutiful in your own life. If you want them to be committed, consistent, and conscientious, then be committed, consistent, and conscientious. In other words, don't merely give them a standard of what you want them

If you want them to be committed, consistent, and conscientious, then be committed, consistent, and conscientious to carry out, but exemplify it in your own life; model for them the people you want them to become.

Speaking of role models, when it comes to marriage, this is one effective way of making a difference in your marriage. In one marriage and family life podcast I was listening to, I learned that instead of trying to change your spouse, work on changing yourself. Another way of putting this is to be the change you want to see in your husband or wife—be a role-model spouse. Notice how the Bible supports this understanding: "You then who teach others, do you not teach yourself? While you preach against stealing, do you steal? You who say that one must not commit adultery, do you commit adultery?"[50]

These questions aren't meant to condemn but to provoke personal examination, to see if you're calling out others on the same points you are failing on (which is hypocrisy). So, if you're going to hold up a standard for your spouse (and others), be sure you are consistently living up to it as well.

> Instead of trying to change your spouse, work on changing yourself.

By the way, this is not to say that you are not to address any wrongs they are doing because you made mistakes also, but when you do, do so in humility, acknowledging your faults and righting those wrongs so that you may be reconciled to each other.

Independence & Individuality

As you already know, which I also mentioned earlier, independence and individuality are fundamental to human growth and development; they go together like a hand-in-glove and should not be surrendered when two people get married. "Neither the husband nor the wife should merge his or her individuality in that of the other."[51] So, don't fall prey to the delusion that if you become more like each other to minimize your differences, then harmony will be achieved. While the two should become "one flesh" (two lives blended as one), they are still two different people, yet the talents and abilities each possesses are to be used to benefit both of them mutually.

Also, "When the wife yields her body and mind to the control of her husband, being passive to his will in all things, sacrificing her conscience, her dignity, and even her identity, she loses the opportunity of exerting that mighty influence for good which she should possess, to elevate her husband."[52] "Neither the husband nor the wife should attempt to exercise over the other an arbitrary control. Do not try to compel each other to yield to your wishes. You cannot do this and retain each other's love."[53]

> "Neither the husband nor the wife should merge his or her individuality in that of the other."[51]

Arbitrary Control and Manipulation

Unfortunately, many husbands and wives resort to manipulation to control each other—to get one's own way or get each other to do what they want—and in some cases, if that doesn't work, there are expressions of anger, withdrawal, or even violence.

Unfortunately, many husbands and wives resort to manipulation to control each other

If one person's mind, preferences, taste buds, or way of life arbitrarily dominate the other person, their personality, talents, and abilities get stifled or suppressed, then the relationship becomes unbalanced, and unhappiness sets in.

Such demanding behavior, entitled mentality, and authoritarian control are forms of oppression and emotional abuse.

Another unfortunate reality is that children raised in this kind of environment are molded with these emotionally destructive traits, which impede the forming of emotionally healthy relationships.

Some people don't perceive this trait in themselves and don't realize how much they are following in their parent's footsteps. Ironically, while they don't want to be controlled, dictated to, or imposed upon, they seek to regulate, dictate, and impose themselves on their spouses—and others—and think it's ok. Sometimes, they mean well and desire not to replicate these inherited traits, yet they are greatly challenged to break the mold, especially in their marriage and parenting relationships.

Furthermore, such mindsets sometimes feel like their spouse is the problem in the marriage and may even feel like a victim when they are actually the one inflicting hurt upon themselves and their partner. Once again, "Neither the husband nor the wife should attempt to exercise over the other an arbitrary control. Do not try to compel each other to yield to your wishes. You cannot do this and retain each other's love. Be kind, patient and forbearing, considerate and courteous. By the grace of God you can succeed in making each other happy, as in your marriage vow you promised to do."[54]

Chapter Five

Adulthood (Maturity)/Mature Love

We've already looked at the fact that we humans go through different stages of development—a child grows through various psychological and physiological changes during youth and teen years into a mature adult male or female. They not only see the world through different lenses but experience it differently, too.

Likewise, marriages go through different stages of development. Generally speaking, it is noted that married couples will go through five different stages, but not all go through them in the very same way or to the same degree or intensity. Let's explore these "5 stages of marriage."[55]

First Stage: In-Love Experience/Enchantment Stage

On December 20th, 2018, USA Today featured an article about a couple who are on "the worlds longest honeymoon." There names are Mike and Anne Howard, and they have documented their accomplishments in their travels on their website, honeytrek.com[56]

> Using Anne's background as a magazine editor and Mike's as a digital media strategist and photographer, we started our couples travel blog to share our seven-continent journey and inspire more people to follow their far-flung dreams. HoneyTrek has grown to be a leading travel blog with over 375,000 followers and has received acclaim from hundreds of media outlets—from *USA Today* to *Lonely Planet*. National Geographic even took notice of our crazy journey and asked us to write their first book on couples' adventure travel, *Ultimate Journeys for Two*. We're proud to say it's a bestseller and published in four languages.[57]

This is certainly not the typical married couple or married life. However, they, like the typical married couple, would start out with the in-love experience or the enchantment stage.

In this stage, we tend to dismiss any perspective of our newfound love that doesn't agree with ours.

This is the stage when emotions are high—you're on cloud nine. You are excited, happy, helpful, and hopeful.

In this stage, we tend to dismiss any perspective of our newfound love that doesn't agree with ours. We gloss over minor differences, even "red flags."

This is the stage where you also look at each other idealistically and are careful not to hurt each other's feelings. As you "endeavor to keep the unity of the spirit in the bonds of peace,"[58] you express kindness, tenderheartedness, and forgiveness toward each other. You even forgo your own desires or preferences to minimize conflicts in your attempt to keep a good thing going.

Inevitably, after the wedding and the honeymoon, this euphoria calms down, and sometime after that, we get to the second stage.

Second Stage: Disappointment/Disenchantment Stage

After the wedding ceremony and honeymoon are over, there is a tendency for disappointment or disenchantment to set in. We have different thoughts and experience different emotions as we seek to fulfill our new roles and responsibilities. Unfortunately, these sometimes express themselves in anger, unkind words, invalidation, insensitivity, indifference, power struggles, mind-over-mind control, and manipulation.

As you can expect, these behaviors engender and intensify conflicts, even though conflicts are common to human relationships. Often, people think their personality differences or upbringing bring the most conflict into their relationships. Still, how well we do or don't handle these differences makes or breaks the bonds between us. "This doesn't mean that differences don't matter. They can be part of what draws two people together and also part of what makes it difficult, at times, to get along. But the part of this over which you have the most control is how the two of you handle whatever differences you have. If you want to have a great relationship, the way you handle differences can matter more than what those differences are."[59]

In getting to or enduring this stage of marriage and resolving marital conflicts, spouses may even wonder if they've made a mistake in marrying. They may even think about the counsels they've negated and neglected. Some Christian couples even question or lose faith in God. They may say something like, "God, why did you let me do this?" or "God, your Word says, 'he who finds a wife finds a good thing,'"[60] or "Lord, your Word says you would 'give me the desires of my heart if I commit myself, wait and put my trust in you'"[61] Of course, such circumstances are the results of our own attitudes, actions, and choices, and not God's doing.

The thoughts and feelings experienced and expressed during the second stage aren't uncommon in relationships but need to become less common and less frequent to maintain harmony and happiness. This is a goal that we should all strive to achieve. Many have achieved this goal, have

First, don't stop fighting for and working on your marriage.

made it through this disappointment stage, through the third stage (which we are about to look at), and have gone on to the "friendship" and "mature love" stages.

However, before talking about those other stages, I would like to pause to encourage you to press forward and not give up if you're in the second stage, the third stage or any other stage of marriage.

Here are three suggestions to help you get through: First, don't stop fighting for and working on your marriage. Don't think that your marriage should or will automatically work out because you love each other or have a high compatibility rate; that's a myth.

Second, be all you can be for your husband or wife

Second, be all you can be for your husband or wife. Things don't get better if you display your worst attitudes and behaviors; they only get worse. While your partner doesn't get everything right, still express gratefulness and thankfulness for what they do. This helps your heart remain tender and open toward each other.

If both of you are hardheaded and hardhearted, then you'll give each other headaches and heartaches by throwing verbal bombs and butting heads continually.

But, if your spouse is violent and abusive, talk to someone who can help. On the other hand, if *you're* violent or abusive, go get help before it's too late.

Third, do not keep yourselves from each other or seek emotional fulfillment in anything or anyone else, whether physical or virtual (like drinking, drugs, gambling, flirting, pornography, or any other vice to find relief). If you do, these will destroy trust and push you further into frustration and depression.

This will also slowly erode the emotional foundation and security of your relationship and erect more emotional barriers between you two, further weakening your bonds and leading you to express contempt for each other.

All of this invites infidelity into the marriage. Still, though, whatever actions you commit is a choice on your part, regardless of how the marriage turns out.

Third, do not keep yourselves from each other or seek emotional fulfillment in anything or anyone else,

Now, let's get back on track with talking about the third of the five stages of marriage.

Third Stage: Obligation/ "Settling" Stage

In this stage, several dynamics occur: couples grow weary from fighting. All the power struggles and manipulative maneuvers have only resulted in more anger, bitterness, frustration, and resentment. They've yet to succeed in changing each other. The things they once enjoyed doing for each other are now done out of obligation or mere duty. They settle in dismay: "It is what it is." "Que sera, sera" (whatever will be, will be), they say.

Though dissatisfied, unhappy, and unfulfilled, they want to maintain their commitment to the marriage—their vows to each other before God and man. They want to do the right thing, and deep down inside, they want the marriage to work out, even though, at times, they are not sure it can.

This stage reminds me of a statement in Gary Chapman's book about the seasons married couples go through:

> "Marriage is not a lifelong Springtime," he says, "But we can come back to the optimism, enthusiasm, and enjoy Spring many times in the course of our lives. We'll inevitably have our seasons of summer, fall, and Winter as well, though not necessarily in that predictable order. As mentioned earlier, the seasons of marriage are not chronological, and thus springtime is not exclusively for newlyweds. The seasons repeat themselves numerous times throughout a marriage, and because we are creatures of choice, we can create new beginnings whenever we desire."[62]

So, there is hope for anyone caught in what may seem like a hopeless situation—an endless fall or a never-ending winter.

Both the fourth and fifth stages of marriage are about hope and living out the "spring" and "summer" time of marriage. Now, let's take a look at these two final stages.

Fourth Stage: "Friendship Love"/In-Love Again Stage

One notable virtue children often display is their ability to make up after a fight. If anyone truly displays what it means to "let not the sun go down on your anger,"[63] it would be them.

The "friendship stage" is about rekindling and fanning the "flames" of love. One of the crucial steps taken to get to this stage is applying a counsel Jesus gave to the church (His "bride"): when she fell out of love with Him. "Remember therefore from where you have fallen, and repent and do the first works."[64] Married couples whose marriages experience a "rebirth," remember when they first started out—the intense emotions they felt for each other. They were curious about each other and desired to see, hear, and spend time together; they expressed tender regard and affection toward each other and the things they hoped to do and accomplish together. They were quick to forgive and willing to please each other.

> One notable virtue children often display is their ability to make up after a fight.

In other words, to move from the "obligation stage" into the "friendship stage" also means they had gone from being resentful, regretful, remorseful, and retaliatory to being redemptive, apologetic, and forgiving. This change of attitude fosters peacemaking, makes room for reconciliation, and makes it safe to connect and do right by each other. As one Bible writer said, "the fruit of righteousness," (evidence of right doing) "is sown in peace of them that make peace."[65]

In Chapter 3, I talked about the wave of emotions and bonding interactions between mothers and children. When married couples go back to the first works, they are, in a sense, returning to "baby stage."

While working on a piece of network equipment at a bank, the manager I was talking with, told me that she believes the empty-nest years are where this type of friendship could be experienced. She thinks this is because the husband and wife are left alone, and their lives no longer involve parenting responsibilities. However, I've learned that married folks stay together during this period if they've bonded well during the years before becoming empty-nesters.

Whether you experience this stage prior to or during the empty-nester years, one thing is for sure: friendship requires that the two be friendly, for those who are to have friends must show themselves to be friendly. Before long, they are talking, sharing, laughing, and playing with each other. Think about how children make friends: they approach with a non-threatening gesture—a wave of the hand to say hi, then, followed by a personal inquiry—what's your name, or do you want to play? Before long, they are talking, sharing, laughing, and playing with each other.

Many preschool experts say that playing is the work children need to do. Through play, children gain developmentally relevant social, emotional, and cognitive abilities. We believe the developmental importance of play doesn't die after childhood, but continues throughout life. Fun and play allow a release of oneself from all the pressures and hassles of being an adult. The relaxed togetherness of playful times is important in the initial development of the bond between two people. That's because when we are engaged in fun through play, we're often relaxed and more ourselves. It's under these conditions that people fall in love — when one sees in the other a relaxed self in the context of fun times together.[66]

Another biblical counsel that is very helpful in transitioning out of the "obligation stage" to this fourth stage of marriage is to "strengthen the things which remain that are ready to die."[67]

To "strengthen the things which remain that are ready to die" requires that you "don't throw out the baby with the bathwater."

I've heard it said by someone whom I don't remember, that we live in a "throw-away culture." If something is broken that can be repaired, instead, we throw it away and get a brand new one, whether we can afford it or not.

To "strengthen the things which remain that are ready to die" requires that you "don't throw out the baby with the bathwater." In other words, you don't take the minor fixable issues that aren't detrimental to the relationship and make them a major. Which can make you feel that your partner is not uniting, cooperating, harmonizing, or supporting you, and then you give up. Instead, you give it a fighting chance by working on fixing the problems that emotionally separate you two from becoming closer, especially the little things that add up and become a mountain. By doing this, you can revive that "love and feeling" you once had for each other, especially if it had gone cold.

In addition, think of your love as a growing plant that must be cultivated and nourished. In a practical sense, like you would grow a plant in a garden, mulch, and water it so it can survive and thrive, so you have to infuse your relationship with things that promote its life.

One way to do this is to pay attention to your words and how you speak to your spouse. "Life and death are in the power of the tongue,"[68] and you can use your words to give your relationship life or death.

"Everything we say is either a bomb or a balm. Bombs destroy. Balm is an aromatic oil or ointment that is soothing and healing. Harsh, cruel, condemning words are like bombs exploding in the hearts of the recipient. Kind, loving, affirming words are like an ointment of healing to the heart of the one who receives them."[69]

Every time my wife and I have a "good talk," things always feel better, and fewer emotional barriers are built between us, which, in turn, strengthens our bonds and increases intimacy.

> "Life and death are in the power of the tongue."

I believe that couples who have gotten to the "friendship stage" have learned to have their speech "seasoned with grace,"[70] and speak more "verbal balms" instead of "verbal bombs." This will not only breathe new life into our hearts, homes, and relationships but also positively impact others we relate to. "Affectionate hearts, truthful, loving words, will make happy families and exert an elevating influence upon all who come within the sphere of their influence." [71]

Fifth Stage: Mature Love/Going Strong and Steady

When a child passes through the various developmental stages into adulthood, much has changed with how they feel, view, and experience life. Similarly, when a husband and wife attain mature love, they feel, view, and experience life together in a different way, too:

> "Affectionate hearts, truthful, loving words, will make happy families and exert an elevating influence upon all who come within the sphere of their influence." [71]

1. They've come through the vicissitudes of life together and are mutually submitted to each other.

2. Their love doesn't die away, even though severely tested.

3. With deep conviction and commitment, they are honoring their marriage vows.

4. Duties/responsibilities are a delight and not a chore or drudgery.

5. They have head-to-heart communication instead of hardheaded conversations (arguments, defensiveness, and monologues).

6. They choose to resolve conflicts and not dissolve them.

7. Now, they collaborate and not just accommodate each other; they choose not to abdicate responsibilities, dictate to, or manipulate each other to get their way.

8. They've learned how to play and have fun with each other.

9. Their relationship more reflects the love portrait of 1 Corinthians 13:4–7, which says, "Love is patient and kind; love does not envy or boast; it is not arrogant or rude. It does not insist on its own way; it is not irritable or resentful; it does not rejoice at wrongdoing, but rejoices with the truth," a love that is forbearing, hopeful, and enduring.

Once again, your marriage may go through all or may only go through some of these stages to the same extent other marriages do. But, if your marriage is going to work out, then you have to *work out* your marriage. Sure, this is easier said than done, but it can be done, has been done, and is being done by many others.

Appendix A

The Marriage Decalogue
Ten Practical, Biblical Principles for Marriage
Maintenance

1. Marriage is a team of two.

Marriage is a team of two. It was instituted by God and among other things, requires mutual honor, mutual submission, love, respect, and sacrifice to make it to the "finish line," and win together. (Genesis 1:27; Matthew 19:4-5; Ephesians 5:22–31; Philippians. 2:3-4; Hebrews 13:3)

2. Speak each other's love language. (1 John 3:18; Hebrews 10:24)

- Words of affirmation
- Quality time
- Physical touch
- Acts of service
- Receiving gifts

3. Be a compliment and not a competition.

- Put away strife and vain glory (conceit, haughty attitude) (Philippians 2:3-4)
- Put away the "do it like me" or the "it's my way or the highway" mentality.

- Maximize on each other's gifts, talents, and abilities (even differences and preferences). (Eph. 4:7–14).

4. Speak verbal balms and not verbal bombs.

- Life and death are in the power of the tongue (used to bless and curse) (Prov. 18:21; James 3:9).

- Gary Chapman: *5 Simple Ways to Strength Your Marriage*, Chapter 1 ("Call a Truce on Verbal Bombs"), Pages 11–13

- Speak pleasant words that are a balm of healing (Prov. 16:24).

5. Be a role model spouse and parent.

- Be the change you want to see in your husband or wife. (Isaiah 1:18)

- Live up to the standard you expect your spouse and children to live up to. (John 13:14, 15; Matt. 7:1–5)

- Role model the value system you want to pass on to your children (Deut. 6:7–9).

- 2 Corinthians 3:18: behold and be changed; the changes in your life can influence your spouse and others around you to change; be the change you want to see in each other.

6. Make a pledge of purity.

- Guard against lust, unclean & immoral content viewing (Ps. 101:3; Matt. 5:28).

- Render to each other due benevolence and minimize long separation. (1 Cor. 7:1–5; 2 Cor. 7:1-5).

- Avoid flirting, jesting, joking, and be careful how you compliment others and not your spouse (Eph. 4:25, 29; 5:3).

7. Choose to resolve and not dissolve conflicts.

- Open communication helps to find real resolutions to make wrongs right. (Isaiah 1:18)

- Avoid long or unnecessary delay (Matt. 5:24, 26).

- To avoid the issue or the person is to choose to dissolve—"silent treatment" is choosing to dissolving the issue.

- Own up to your wrongs (James 5:16).

- Note: Sometimes rights or preferences have to be relinquished to resolve conflicts.

- Put aside pride and avoid condescending, contemptuous remarks or attitudes, and contention and strife will cease (Prov. 13:10; 22:10).

8. Choose confrontation and not retaliation.

- Do it prayerfully, personally, promptly, privately, and purposefully. (Matthew 5:23–26; 18:15)

- Appropriately include third parties (Matt. 18:15–17).

- Galatians 6:1 Purpose and spirit when confronting someone.

- To restore the relationship, make things right or better.

- Approach the person or the issue with humility.

9. Have winsome arguments.

- Attack the issue, not the person (Eccles. 4:9, 12).

- Don't be hasty to speak or be defensive; "Seek first to understand then to be understood" (James 1:19).

- Own up to your wrongs (James 5:16).

- Speak a soft answer to turn away wrath (aggravation, irritation) (Prov. 15:1).

- Note: A soft answer may mean "biting your tongue," saying sorry today, but talking it over tomorrow.

10. Exercise forgiveness and reconciliation.

Note: The beginning of reconciliation is an acknowledgment and confession of wrongs, then, the experience of forgiveness.

- Don't go to bed angry; make up as soon as you can (Eph. 4:26).

- Be kind, tenderhearted, and forgiving to each other (Eph. 4:32).

- Confess faults one to another and pray for each other; makes room for healing and reconciliation (James 5:16).

- Peacemaking fosters right actions (James 3:18).

Appendix B

Parenting/Child Guidance

1. Carefully consider the cost of parenting.

- Besides finances, it requires much spiritual, mental, emotional, and physical energy to raise a child/children properly. Luke 14:28-30; Proverbs 24:3

2. God's Gift, God's Heritage.

- A precious gift & a sacred trust. Psalm 127:3

3. Be Attentive to Early Childhood Years.

- Training should start with the early childhood years, as from ages 0-7, 100% of the adult brain is developed, though not fully matured. It is during these years that a character foundation is formed. Proverbs 22:6

- Children live what they learn and are changed by it, so limit screen time (TV, video games, and other content viewing). 2 Corinthians 3:18

4. Role model the value system you want your children to adopt.

- Incorporate & exemplify ethical, moral, and biblical values and principles into everyday living. Deuteronomy 6:3-7

5. Portray the standards you profess to believe in.

- Live up to the standards you expect your children to live up to. For example, if you want them to be courteous, productive, and clean, then be courteous, productive, and clean. Romans 2:21-25; John 13:14,15; Matthew 7:1-5

6. Do not neglect proper discipline.

- Reproof and correction are a part of life. This is apart of applying "the rod of correction." If you spare this "rod," you'll spoil the child. Proverbs 22:15; 29:15. Harsh and unreasonable punishment or too little discipline can lead to rebellion or bratty behaviors.

7. Valid Your Child/Children

- Validating your child is a positive way to boost their self-worth. Encourage them with words of approval and looks of love. Commend their good behaviors and accomplishments and not only call attention to their wrongs and misbehavior.

8. Sibling Rivalry

- Guard against favoritism, which can lead to bad relationships between siblings. Consider the stories of Isaac, his wife Rebekah, and their sons (Jacob & Esau) Genesis 27:1-45; Jacob with his son Joseph and his twelve brothers. Genesis chapter 37. To not show favoritism does not mean all children get equal amount of means, or even the same treatment in every particular or be apart of everything all the time, especially when they are of different ages, levels of maturity, and interests. You have to relate to them accordingly.

9. Study your family tree & personality traits.

• Inherited & cultivated tendencies, or the "sins of the fathers," run in families. The stories involving Laban, Rebekah, Jacob, and the kings of the Bible exemplify how ruinous certain family traits can be. Genesis chapters 27 & 29-31; Exodus 20:5-6; 1Kings chapters 15 &16; 2 Kings chapter 15).

• Understand your child's personality and adapt approaches that better fit their personality.

• Consider the twelve characters of Jacob's children; each one represents one of us. Genesis 49:1-28

10. Be careful of what type of parenting style you adopt.

• Avoid the indulgent, passive, or "not adulting" parenting style. This can be destructive to others besides your child/children. Consider the story of Eli and his sons on this point. 1 Samuel chapters 2-4.

• Avoid being dedicated to your vocation (work or career) to the neglect of spending consistent, quality family time.

• Also, strike a balance between authoritative and nurturing parenting.

- Finally, guide your children to deal with family, cultural, or traditional practices that conflict with your family's values: Help them to be their own advocates.

Appendix C

The Courtship Challenge

1. Preparation is a principle of life and is vital to the success of any venture, including marriage.

- Success or failure in any endeavor depends upon different things; one of them is preparation. The growing-up years are the period in which a person is growing and maturing toward adulthood, and are also the years of preparation for courtship and marriage. Whatever manners, morals, principles, or etiquette adopted, will influence adult life and impact relationships. Additionally, courtship is also a period to get a better sense of who your prospect is and is not a guarantor for marriage. (Luke 14:28-30; 1 Corinthians 13:11)

2. Don't let your emotions lead you.

- Invite God into your experience. (Proverbs 3:5) In all your ways acknowledge him and he shall direct your paths. He gives enlightenment and protection; He gives grace and honor; no good thing will he withhold from those who walk uprightly. (Psalm 84:11)

3. Check out your prospect's social circle.

- How a person treats close family members, friends, neighbors, and coworkers is a good indicator of who they are and how they would treat you. Beauty is what beauty does. "A person who has friends must themselves be friendly." (Proverbs 18:24)

4. Check out your prospect's religious beliefs.

- Many people govern their way of life by their religious beliefs. For example, the things they do or don't do, the type of entertainment they prefer, places they go or don't go to, the music they listen or don't listen to, and movies they watch or don't watch; these and other lifestyle choices are usually based on some religious philosophy (even for those who don't profess religion). Understanding this helps to avoid unnecessary conflicts and misunderstandings about certain preferences they have or choices they make. (Proverbs 4:7; Amos 3:3)

5. Check out your prospect's spending habits/money management.

- Many divorces are caused by irresponsible spending or mismanagement of the family finances. The prodigal son Bible story demonstrates what can happen when the family resources are squandered. (Luke 15:11-16) Also, a love affair with money is harmful to relationships. (1 Timothy 6:10)

6. Seek premarital counseling.

- Where there is no council, plans are disappointed; but through many councils, plans can better be established and succeed; for among many counselors there is wisdom. (Proverbs 15:22; Proverbs 24:3, Job 12:12)

7. Don't dismiss "red flags."

- Just as habits strengthen with age, so "red flags" tend to magnify in relationships over time. It's a myth to thing that someone will change after they get married. Proverbs 22:3 help us to understand that the prudent person foresees trouble and take precautions, but the gullible blindly go on and suffer the consequences.

8. Study your family tree and theirs.

- Certain character traits run in families, AKA "sins of the fathers," generational curses, or strongholds. Having this knowledge can help steer you away from unnecessary life and relationship troubles. In the bible narratives of Laban, Rebekah, and Jacob, we see the family trait of deception. (see Genesis chapters 27 & 29-31.) Also, the kings of the Bible exemplify how ruinous certain family traits can be. (see 1 Kings chapters 15 &16; 2 Kings chapter 15).

9. Discuss roles and responsibilities.

- Two can't "walk together" without agreeing on how they are going to live and manage a household together. One area of relationship where this becomes very important is parenting because when children are born into the family, they affect the family dynamics; routines and responsibilities get rearranged. (Amos 3:3)

10. Miscellaneous

- Talk about sleeping routine, eating habits, educational interests & pursuits, goals, family planning, conflict resolution, and so on. "Wisdom is the principal thing; therefore get wisdom: and with all thy getting get understanding." (Proverbs 4:7.)

Citation Page

1. New York Times, Feb 2, 2022: It's a Boom Year for Brides and Grooms https://www.nytimes.com/2022/02/04/fashion/weddings/wedding-boom-year.html

2. Pew Research Center, November 6, 2019, Marriage & Cohabitation in the US, By Juliana Menasce Horowitz, Nikki Graf, and Gretchen Livingston https://www.pewresearch.org/social-trends/2019/11/06/why-people-get-married-or-move-in-with-a-partner/#:~:text=Among%20married%20and%20cohabiting%20adults,major%20factor%20in%20their%20decision.

3. Howard J. Marksman, Scott M. Stanley, Susan L. Blumberg, Fighting for Your Marriage: Chapter 1, Understanding the Risk on the Road to Lasting Love, Page 19. (2010)

4. Debra Paget Smith, Confronting Without Offending: Biblical Confrontation and Conflict Management Styles, page 29-69 (2009)

5. Fox News, March, 15 2023, Britt Briner, Family as cornerstone of society: How to celebrate the birthday that means the most. https://www.foxnews.com/lifestyle/family-cornerstone-society-celebrate-birthday-means-most

6. Ellen G. White, Adventist Homes: Atmosphere of the Home, Chapter 1, Page 15. (May 8, 1952)

7. Howard J. Marksman, Scott M. Stanley, Susan L. Blumberg, Fighting for Your Marriage: Playing Together, Chapter 11, page 258 (2010)

8. Exodus 20:5, KJV

9. 2 Corinthians, 13:5 KJV

10. James 1:8 KJV

11. 2 Corinthians 10:12; Acts 19:15 KJV

12. Luke 12:15, KJV

13. Why prioritizing motherhood in first 3 years is critical: Rachel Nania, May 19, 2017 https://wtop.com/parenting/2017/05/why-prioritizing-motherhood-in-the-first-three-years-is-critical/#:~:text=A%20mother's%20physical%20and%20emotional,the%20child's%20future%20well%2Dbeing.

14. How a Mother's Love Changes a Child's Brain: Joseph Castro, January 30, 2012 https://www.livescience.com/18196-maternal-support-child-brain.html

15. https://www.brookings.edu/articles/the-unique-power-of-dads-in-childhood-development-during-a-pandemic-and-beyond/

16. https://www.zerotothree.org/resource/the-daddy-factor-how-fathers-support-development/

17. Ellen G. White, Testimonies to the Church, Vol, 3:Love and Sympathy at Home, page 532.

18. Ellen G. White, Testimonies to the Church, Vol, 3:Love and Sympathy at Home, page 532.

19. 1Corinthians 13:10-11 NKJV.

20. Pew Research, November 6, 2019. By Juliana Menasce Horowitz, Nikki Graf and Gretchen Livingston

    https://www.pewresearch.org/social-trends/2019/11/06/why-people-get-married-or-move-in-with-apartner/#:~:text=Among%20married20and20cohabiting20adults,major%20factor%20in%20their%20decision.

21. Gary Chapman, The 5 Love Languages: Keeping the Love Tank Full, page 19, (1992-2015)

22. Ellen G White, Adventist Homes: The Great Decision, Chapter 6, page 43. (1952)

23. Proverbs 3:5 NKJV

24. John 4:4-29 NKJV

25. Like 7:36-50 KJV

26. John 2:1-12 NKJV

27. 2 Corinthians 3:18 NKJV

28. Proverbs 11:14; 15:22 KJV

29. Amos 3:3 NKJV

30. Ellen G White, Fundamentals of Christian Education: Courtship and Marriage, pages 104, 105.

31. Ellen G. White, Adventist Homes: The Great Decision, Chapter 6, page 43. (1952)

32. Ellen G. White, Adventist Homes: Compatibility, chapter 11, page 84. (May 8, 1952)

33. Howard J. Marksman, Scott M. Stanley, Susan L. Blumberg, Fighting for your Marriage: Chapter 1, page 25. (2010)

34. 5 Simple Ways to Strengthen Your Marriage: Discover and Speak Each Other's Love Language, page 44. (2020)

35. Gary Chapman, The 5 Love Languages: Words of Affirmation, Chapter 4, Page 37-54. (2015)

36. Gary Chapman, The 5 Love Languages: Quality Time, Chapter 4, Page 55-74. (2015)

37. Gary Chapman, The 5 Love Languages: Receiving Gifts, Chapter 4, Page 75-89. (2015)

38. Gary Chapman, The 5 Love Languages: Acts of Services, Chapter 4, Page 90-106. (2015)

39. Gary Chapman, The 5 Love Languages: Physical Touch, Chapter 4, Page 107-117.(2015)

40. Gary Chapman, 5 Simple Ways to Strengthen Your Marriage: Discover and Speak Each Other's Love Language, page 40-46. (2020)

41. Ellen G. White, Adventist Homes: Compatibility, Chapter 12, Page 83

42. How to Handle Conflict Effectively, February 19, 2020, Darlene Lancer, JD, LMFT https://www.psychologytoday.com/us/blog/toxic-relationships/202002/how-handle-conflict-effectively

43. How to Handle Conflict Effectively, February 19, 2020, Darlene Lancer, JD, LMFT https://www.psychologytoday.com/us/blog/toxic-relationships/202002/how-handle-conflict-effectively

44. Debra Smith Pagues, Confronting Without Offending: The Goal of Confrontation, page 16. (2009)

45. Debra Smith Pagues, Confronting Without Offending: Winning With Deborah (July 22, 2018) https://youtu.be/Zd7L9W8G_Io

46. Gary Chapman, 5 Simple Ways to Strengthen Your Marriage: Call a Truce on Throwing Verbal Bombs, Chapter 1, page 11-12. (2020)

47. https://files.firstthingsfirst.org/why-early-childhood-matters/the-first-five-years

48. Gary Chapman, The 4 Seasons of Marriage: Adapting to Changing Seasons, page 6. (2005)

49. Gary Chapman, The 4 Seasons of Marriage: Adapting to Changing Seasons:, page 7. (2005)

50. John 13:14-15; Romans 2:21–22 (ESV)

51. Ellen G. White, The Testimony on Sexual Behavior, page 26.

52. The Review and Herald, September 26, 1899.

53. Ellen G. White, The Testimony on Sexual Behavior: Individuality chapter 3, page 26.

54. Ellen G. White, The Testimony on Sexual Behavior: Individuality chapter 3, page 26.

55. Roger K Allen, PhD. Creating a Happy Marriage and Loving Relationship: Stages of Marriage Satisfaction, Presentation 3.

56. https://www.usatoday.com/picturegallery/travel/destinations/2018/12/20/honeytrek-couple-worldslongesthoneymoon/2373446002/#:~:text=Cusco%20in20Peru., HoneyTrek,HoneyTrek

57. https://www.honeytrek.com/about/

58. Eph. 4:2–3, 32 KJV

59. Fighting For Your Marriage Page 25-26. (2010)

60. Proverbs 18:22 KJV

61. Psalm 37:4 KJV

62. Four Seasons of Marriage page22, par 2. (2005)

63. Ephesians 4:26 KJV

64. Revelation 2:4-5 KJV

65. James 3:18 KJV

66. Fighting for your marriage: Playing Together, Page 258. (2010)

67. Revelation 3:2, 3 KJV

68. Proverbs 18:21 KJV

69. Gary Chapman, 5 Simple Ways to Strength Your Marriage: Call a Truce on Throwing Verbal Bombs, page 11 (2020)

70. Colossians 4:6 KJV

71. Ellen G. White, Adventist Home page 50